Are you brave or bashful?

The Bible is full of interesting people. This book takes a closer look at some of them—and at the surprising things that happen to them.

Some start out bashful—and end up as heroes.

Others try too hard to be brave—and fall flat on their faces.

You'll read about a lady general, a noisy beggar, a bashful prince, and many other characters.

And you'll learn that God has a place in His plan for you, whether you're brave or bashful.

Other books by William Coleman . . .

Kings and Kritters

Far Out Facts

The
BRAVE
and the
BASHFUL

Surprising Stories from the Bible

William L. Coleman

Illustrated by
Nick Englehardt
and
Loran Berg

Published by Chariot Books™,
an imprint of David C. Cook Publishing Co.

David C. Cook Publishing Co., Elgin, Illinois 60120
David C. Cook Publishing Co., Weston, Ontario

THE BRAVE AND THE BASHFUL

Design by Loran Berg
Illustrations by Nick Engelhardt and Loran Berg

First Printing, 1989
Printed in the United States of America
93 92 91 90   2 3 4 5

All Scripture quotations in this publication are from the Holy Bible,
New International Version. Copyright © 1973, 1978, 1984, International
Bible Society.

Library of Congress Cataloging-in-Publication Data

Coleman, William L.
  The brave and the bashful : surprising stories from the Bible / William
L. Coleman; illustration by Nick Engelhardt and Loran Berg.
      p. cm.
  ISBN 0-89191-988-0
  1. Bible stories, English. I. Title.

BS551.2.C63 1989   88-37131
220.9'505—dc19   CIP

CONTENTS

THE SUN STOOD STILL

On the day the LORD gave the Amorites over to Israel, Joshua said to the LORD in the presence of Israel:

"O sun, stand still over Gibeon,
O moon, over the Valley of Aijalon." . . .
The sun stopped in the middle of the sky and delayed going down about a full day.

Joshua 10:12, 13b

WHAT'S IT ABOUT?

Sometimes bad weather will help you escape a task. (For example, you can't mow the lawn when it's raining!) But brave Joshua wanted daylight to get his task done. His surprising request had amazing results.

★For the whole story, read Joshua 10:1-15 in your Bible.

Good Fighters

As Joshua and the Israelites were conquering Canaan, the land God had promised to them, they came near the city of Gibeon.

The Gibeonites were famous as good fighters. They

were also smart enough to make peace with the Israelite invaders.

But their peace treaty with Israel angered the kings of five other cities. Those five kings wanted to attack Gibeon.

Five Kings

The kings of Jerusalem
　　　　Hebron
　　　　Jarmuth
　　　　Lachish
　　　　Eglon
joined forces for the battle.

The five were called the Amorite kings.

Pony Express

Quickly the Gibeonites sent messengers to Joshua at his camp at Gilgal. "Help! Come and rescue us!" they demanded.

Marching Orders

Joshua pulled his army together and they began a march toward Gibeon to help their friends. They knew that they might be outnumbered, but went anyway. They marched all night.

A Brief Biography

Joshua was the son of Nun.
 He worked for a while as a spy.
 He followed Moses as leader of Israel.
 He was 110 years old when he died.

Guarantee by God

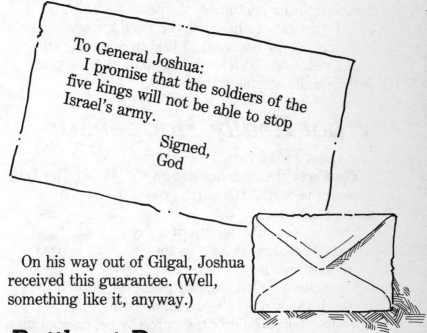

To General Joshua:
 I promise that the soldiers of the five kings will not be able to stop Israel's army.

Signed,
God

 On his way out of Gilgal, Joshua received this guarantee. (Well, something like it, anyway.)

Battle at Dawn

Israel surprised the five Amorite armies the next morning. After a huge fight, the Jews won, and started chasing the surviving warriors.

Raining Rocks?

As the armies of the five kings ran away, God sent hailstones shooting out of the sky. More soldiers died in the storm than in the battle.

No Light Bulbs

As the fighting continued, the Jews began running out of daylight. To help get the job done while they could still see, Joshua asked God to make the sun stand still. God did. The day lasted longer so that Joshua could complete the battle.

What Really Happened?

Can the sun stand still?

The Facts: The sun doesn't go around the earth. The earth goes around the sun.

The Problem: The length of a day would not change as long as the earth kept moving.

The Solution: God stopped whatever needed to be stopped: the sun, or the earth, or both.

A Question: Wouldn't the universe get messed up if a star and a planet stopped moving?

Answer: Certainly. But if He wanted to, God could break the rules of the universe and still keep everything in order.

Solution #2: Maybe the sun and earth kept on moving, and God merely bent the light rays to make the daylight last longer.

Was Joshua Wrong?

Well, uh, yes. That is, no. Would you believe, maybe?

Joshua saw the daylight continue. It looked like the sun stood still. The miracle of a longer day definitely happened.

Did Joshua know that the earth revolves around the sun? Maybe we can ask him that when we get to heaven.

Joshua's Faith

Joshua had a bold faith. When he asked God to make the sun stand still, he knew his cause was right, and believed God could make the day last longer if He wanted.

Who?

1. Who marched against Gibeon?
2. Who were the Amorite kings?
3. Who led Israel?
4. Who asked for the longer day?

(Answers: 1. The five kings 2. The five kings 3. Joshua 4. Joshua)

Figure It Out

Did you know that *Gilgal* spelled backwards is *laglig?*

Pick One

Which two of these statements are true?

1. God can do anything He wants to in nature.

2. When the sun stops, all the sundials need to be repaired.

3. When God makes a promise, He finds a way to keep it.

4. Wars should never be fought at night.

5. Armies that fight in the sun could get skin damage.

(Answers: 1, 3)

THE LADY WAS A GENERAL

Deborah, a prophetess, the wife of Lappidoth, was leading Israel at that time. . . . She sent for Barak son of Abinoam . . . and said to him, "The LORD, the God of Israel, commands you: 'Go, take with you ten thousand men of Naphtali and Zebulun and lead the way to Mount Tabor. I will lure Sisera, the commander of Jabin's army, with his chariots and his troops to the Kishon River and give him into your hands.' "

Barak said to her, "If you go with me, I will go: but if you don't go with me, I won't go;"

Judges 4:4, 6-8

WHAT'S IT ABOUT?

Men weren't the only brave people in the Bible. Two women were the heroines of this battle against Israel's enemies!

★For the complete story, read Judges 4 in your Bible.

The Bad Guys

King Jabin of Hazor	General Sisera	The Israelites, who had sinned against God

Israel Apologizes

After twenty years of being pushed around by King Jabin, Israel told God they were sorry they had sinned. They wanted God to forgive them and get the Canaanites off their backs.

Chariots of Iron

The speed with which the Canaanites of Hazor could strike made them a tremendous military power. Their 900 "iron chariots" were not made entirely of iron, but had iron in some of the parts, such as the wheels.

Famous Prophetess

Name: Deborah, wife of Lappidoth
Occupations: prophetess, judge, general
Address: Deborah's Palm Tree
Claim to Fame: only female judge in the Book of Judges
Height and Weight: unknown
Eyes: two
Hair: yes

The Lady Was a Judge

Even before the big battle, Deborah had already been leading the nation of Israel. They came to her to settle disputes.

The Tree with a Name

Instead of presiding over a majestic courtroom, Deborah judged cases while sitting outside under a large palm tree. The tree became known as the "Palm of Deborah."

Two Generals

Barak told Deborah he would not lead Israel's army of ten thousand men unless she led it with him. Deborah agreed.

Mud Wrestling

The Jewish army climbed down the side of Mount Tabor, ready to attack the chariots of Hazor. Just as they arrived, the waters of the River Kishon rose (probably because of a sudden rainstorm) and made the chariots useless (Judges 5:21). The Jews chased the enemy and caught them in the mud.

What Did Deborah Do?

How did Deborah lead the army of Israel?

1. Did she ride a horse and swing her sword in all directions?

2. Did she ride in a chariot, shouting orders and maybe shooting an arrow now and then?

3. Did she stand on Mount Tabor, yelling orders and sending an occasional messenger to her troops?

4. Did she go home and watch it all on TV?

No one knows for sure. But if you guessed number 4, you probably need a nap.

Milk and Cookies?

Sisera, the enemy general, managed
to escape to the tent of the woman
Jael. He felt safe there because Jael's
husband's people were not at war
with the Canaanites.

Jael gave the general some milk and put a warm
blanket over him (Judges 4:19). Soon he was
comfortably asleep.

An Ugly End

Jael risked her life to defeat Israel's enemy. While
Sisera was in dreamland, Jael swiftly hammered a
tent peg through his temple. She hit it so hard it
went through his head and stuck in the ground. It
was an ugly way to go.

You Can Be Like Deborah

None of the four guys was really Buck's good friend.
He was just hanging around with them for the day.
Buck had a good time with them for a while. But as
they were walking through the grocery store, each
of the other boys would stop just long enough to
stuff food in his pocket.

Buck knew what they were doing
was wrong. Something in the back of
his mind told him to get away. It was
a hard decision. Buck knew the guys
would just call him a chicken. But he
couldn't be part of what they were
doing.

In an instant, Buck turned around and walked out the side door. Just moments after he left, the store's security guard stopped the other four guys.

When we hear God telling us what to do, we need to obey, even if it's hard. Deborah may not have wanted to lead an army. But she obeyed, and by God's power the Canaanite forces were defeated.

SINK OR SWIM!

When the disciples saw him walking on the lake, they were terrified. "It's a ghost," they said, and cried out in fear.

But Jesus immediately said to them: "Take courage! It is I. Don't be afraid."

"Lord, if it's you," Peter replied, "tell me to come to you on the water."

"Come," He said.

Matthew 14:26-29a

WHAT'S IT ABOUT?

Would you feel afraid in a boat on a stormy night? Or if you thought you saw a ghost? In the middle of this spooky time, Peter did one of the bravest things of all.

★For the whole story, read Matthew 14:22-33 in your Bible.

The Great Getaway

Jesus had just finished feeding five thousand men plus women and children (a possible total of over ten thousand people). The crowd hated to see Jesus and His disciples leave.

Jesus was trying to organize an orderly getaway.

Shipped Them Out

Jesus hustled the disciples into a boat and sent them out on the lake.

Many of the disciples had been fishermen, and were no strangers to boats. This boat was probably a fishing vessel just large enough for the twelve of them to squeeze on board. It may have been a sailboat, or a boat powered by oars.

Mountain Climbing

After Jesus convinced the crowd to leave, He looked for a place to be alone and talk to God.

Rocking the Boat

As it grew dark, Jesus continued to pray on the mountain. Meanwhile, the boat had gone far from land and into stormy weather. Winds were smacking against the small boat and tossing it around.

Getting Seasick

The storm probably began in the evening (possibly 6:00 p.m.). Jesus came to help them during the "fourth watch," between 3:00 and 6:00 a.m. The disciples had been tossed around by the waves for at least nine hours before help arrived.

Jesus Takes a Hike

When Jesus saw the raging sea and understood the trouble the disciples were in, He decided to help them. He didn't need to take a boat or go swimming to get there. He just walked on top of the water.

Maybe he pulled part of his robe up over his ears to keep out the spray. Or maybe the storm moved aside so that not a drop touched him.

A Spooky Feeling

The disciples were frightened enough by the storm and the darkness. Now they got a double shock. When they glimpsed the figure of Jesus walking on the water, they thought He was a ghost. They let out a frightened yell.

Most of us would have reacted the same way.

Familiar Voice

Jesus spoke up and told the disciples not to panic. Peter recognized the voice. He knew who was standing on the water, and called Him Lord.

Come Walk with Me

Jesus invited Peter to step out of the boat and stand on the water with Him.

Let's hear loud applause for Peter! Not many of us would have gotten out of that boat. Peter believed Jesus and put his faith into action.

Bubble, Bubble, Bubble

No sooner had Peter gotten out of the boat than he noticed the howling wind. The storm had not stopped. Peter broke into a sweat and began to sink.

Help!

Peter called out for Jesus to rescue him—and fast!

Lending a Hand

Quickly Jesus stretched out His hand and Peter grabbed hold of it. Both men returned to the boat safely.

On the way, Jesus explained that Peter was safe as long as he had faith. When he began to doubt, the water no longer supported him and he started to sink.

Floating Church

As Jesus entered the boat, the wind quit blowing. The vessel became a church as the men started worshiping God.

They had seen a miracle.

They had seen the power of God.

They had seen the Son of God.

And they knew He cared about them.

Check the Numbers

1. How many people did Jesus feed?
2. How long were the disciples in the boat before Jesus came along?
3. At what time did Jesus walk on the water?

(Answers: 1. Five to ten thousand 2. At least nine hours 3. Between 3:00 and 6:00 a.m.)

What Did Jesus Prove?

1. He knew where there were rocks in the lake to step on.
2. He owned the first pair of balloon sandals.
3. He was a good water skier.
4. He had God's power over the forces of nature.

(Answer: The first three answers are weird.)

Speak Up!

What do you think of Peter in this story? Is he brave or bashful? Explain your answer.

HIGH-RISE BUILDERS

Now the whole world had one language and a common speech. As men moved eastward, they found a plain in Shinar and settled there. . . .
Then they said, "Come, let us build ourselves a city, with a tower that reaches to the heavens, so that we may make a name for ourselves and not be scattered over the face of the whole earth."
Genesis 11:1, 2, 4

WHAT'S IT ABOUT?
The people in this story were not afraid of heights! In fact, they were a bit too brave. . . .

★For the complete account, read Genesis 11:1-9 in your Bible.

Everyone Knew It

Originally there was only one language. There was no need for interpreters, translators, or subtitles! We aren't sure what that first language was.

Where Was the Tower?

Shinar is believed to have been in Babylonia (present-day Iraq). The people were moving eastward when they decided to stop and settle in this fertile area.

A City-Tower Complex

The people decided to build homes, shops, and possibly palaces. They wanted a spectacular tower as part of the city to impress everyone with how clever they were. They probably also wanted to impress God.

Baking Bricks

Bricks were shaped out of mud, and often just left to harden in the sunlight. However the bricks in this story were baked in ovens, called kilns, to make them better-looking and stronger.

Normally straw was mixed into the mud before it was baked, in order to strengthen the brick.

Often prisoners or slaves were given the job of making bricks.

Why Bother?

Why did the people go to all the work of baking bricks instead of just building with stone?

1. Stones may have been hard to collect in this area.

2. Bricks, with their uniform size and shape, may have been easier to use—and more attractive. After all, they did want to impress everyone.

Later the Babylonians made bricks with figures on them, such as lions or deer.

Sticky Stuff

The builders used mortar or tar instead of clay to help the bricks stick together. This added strength to the structure and gave it a first-class look.

Can You Say Ziggurat?

Later Babylonian temple towers were called ziggurats. They looked like mountains or pyramids with stair-stepped sides. This tower may have looked like a ziggurat.

How Tall Was It?

At this time, most structures were probably only one or two stories high. A few special buildings would have been larger, though. Would this have been ten stories high, or twenty? We'll have to guess on that one.

The builders must have known that their building could not reach the stars. "A tower that reaches to the heavens" was an expression meaning the building was extremely tall.

A Little Too Brave

These proud people thought they were really something. By building this huge tower and beautiful city, they would prove how important they were.

God to the Rescue

Blow the whistle. Call the rescue squad. These people need help!

They were starting to think they were so great that they didn't need anyone—not even God.

God decided to act quickly before their attitude got worse.

Gobbledygook

Bam! God suddenly gave the people different languages. Did every person have a separate language? Maybe. Certainly each group spoke differently. Possibly one group spoke Chinese, another Greek, a third Hebrew, and maybe many more.

They all thought the others sounded like gobbledygook.

Shut Down

Construction stopped. The brick bakers walked off the job. The architects couldn't understand one another. Mud mixers left their mud piles.

Why Was It Called Babel?

We aren't sure why this area was given the name "Babel." In Babylonian, the name means "gateway to a god," but it also sounds like the Hebrew for "confusion," or a place of confusion.

Tell Us How!

1. How did the people make bricks?
2. How did God help them?
3. How did God scatter the people?

(Answers: 1. Baked them. 2. Scattered them. 3. Gave them many languages.)

Pick One

What is the point of this story?
1. God hates skyscrapers.
2. Never build without praying about it.
3. Never use cheap bricks.
4. If you become too proud, you may start thinking you don't need God.

THE BRAVE SERVANT

Now bands from Aram had gone out and had taken captive a young girl from Israel, and she served Naaman's wife. She said to her mistress, "If only my master would see the prophet who is in Samaria! He would cure him of his leprosy."

II Kings 5:2, 3

WHAT'S IT ABOUT?

In an enemy land, this brave young girl from Israel acted with love—and started good things happening.

★For the whole story, read II Kings 5 in your Bible.

Medical Chart

Patient: Commander Naaman, officer in Army of Aram, or Syria.

Condition: Patient had leprosy. Exact nature of this illness unknown. Many types of skin diseases were called leprosy.

Treatment: None. Patient was expected to die.

What's Her Name?

The heroine is a young girl from Israel, taken
captive by Aramean soldiers in a border raid. We
know she worked in Naaman's house, serving his
wife. But we don't know her name.

Amazing Attitude

When the girl heard of Naaman's illness, she wanted
to find a way to help. She could have been bitter
about being stolen from her homeland; certainly she
felt sad. But she took this opportunity to help her
captors anyway.

The Elisha Clinic

The slave girl recommended that Naaman travel to
Samaria, where the prophet Elisha lived.

One King Helps

When Naaman told the king of Aram about going to
Israel, the king was thrilled. He wanted his star
soldier cured. He even wrote a personal letter to the
king of Israel, asking for his help.

The Other King Sweats

"What does he want? Are they trying to pick a
fight?" wondered the king of Israel. He knew there
was no cure for leprosy. He tore his clothes and
probably sweated a lot. The king was a nervous
wreck.

Tearing Clothes

This was an old custom among the Jews. When they were overcome with an emotion such as grief or sorrow or fear, they might tear part of their garments.

If you tried this custom today, your mother would not appreciate it.

Oops!

The king of Aram assumed that if someone in Israel could cure leprosy, the king of Israel would certainly know all about it.

But neither king really knew what was going on.

Rumors Spread Fast

Word got around that the king had torn his clothes. When Elisha heard that the king was frantic, he sent a message: "Send Naaman to me."

RX

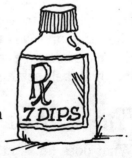

Naaman's horses and chariots paraded over to Elisha's house. Elisha didn't bother to come out. He just sent a prescription: seven dips in the Jordan River would erase the leprosy.

No further checkups necessary. The medical file would be closed.

Naaman Throws a Fit

Naaman thought it sounded like a lousy way to get cured. Why didn't Elisha come out and do a dance, throw chicken beaks in the air, or recite a rock-and-roll song?

The commander was miffed. The Abana and Pharpar Rivers in Damascus were better-looking rivers, he thought. The very idea of dipping in the Jordan disgusted him. Yecch!

Calm Down!

Naaman's servants tried to reason with him. They pointed out that if Elisha had asked him to do a tough task, Naaman would have acted immediately. Why not do an easy task and live?

Gone to the River

Naaman decided to obey Elisha's orders. Seven quick dunks sounded reasonable—especially when the alternative was probably death.

Baby Soft

When Naaman finished dipping seven times, he came up with young, smooth skin. There was no trace of the disease. He was healthy and so-o-o-o happy. Hurray for God!

No Gifts

Naaman wanted to give presents to Elisha because of the miracle that had happened. Elisha refused. Naaman's thanks to God was payment enough.

Straighten Them Out

Unscramble the following words:
1. Danjor
2. Manana
3. Sleahi
4. Camsudas
5. Reilas

(Answers: 1. Jordan 2. Naaman 3. Elisha 4. Damascus 5. Israel)

You Say It

Who tore the king's clothes, and why?

(Answer: The king of Israel tore his own clothes because he thought the king of Aram was trying to start a war.)

Mary's Room

Mary's mother told her to clean up her room, and Mary was mad.

It wasn't that Mary didn't like clean bedrooms. She did. And it wasn't that Mary minded doing the work. She just didn't like to be told what to do.

So Mary put it off. She stayed messy just to be stubborn.

Naaman was like Mary. He needed to be healed, but he didn't like to be told what to do. Only after he squashed down his pride did he find the cure he wanted.

THE BASHFUL PRINCE

Now Moses was tending the flock of Jethro his father-in-law, the priest of Midian, and he led the flock to the far side of the desert and came to Horeb, the mountain of God. There the angel of the LORD appeared to him in flames of fire from within a bush. Moses saw that though the bush was on fire it did not burn up.

Exodus 3:1, 2

WHAT'S IT ABOUT?

Moses was bashful. The former prince thought he was no good for anything but watching sheep—until he had a strange experience by a bush.

★For the whole story, read Exodus 2—4 in your Bible.

Baby Boom

At the time Moses was born, the Jews had been living in Egypt for four hundred years, and their numbers were growing. The Egyptians began to worry that the Jews might fight against them.

33

Dirty Work

To keep the Jews under control in the land, the Egyptian pharaoh made them slaves. They were forced to lug loads of mortar and carry cases of bricks.

Word Doctor

The word *pharaoh* is a title that means *king*. The ancient Egyptians considered pharaohs to be gods. When the pharaohs were buried, most of them were made into mummies. We don't know the name of the pharaoh in the Exodus account. The Bible just calls him *Pharaoh*.

From Slave to Prince

Though he was the son of a Hebrew slave, Moses was raised in Pharaoh's palace as the Pharaoh's adopted grandson. How did this happen? To control the slave population, Pharaoh had ordered all newborn Hebrew boys tossed into the Nile River. Moses' mother put him in the river—in a small boat made from a papyrus basket.

Pharaoh's daughter found the baby afloat in the river and decided to adopt him. She knew the baby was a Jew, but she kept him anyway.

Murder!

Though Moses grew up in a royal palace, he never forgot his own people were slaves. One day he saw an Egyptian beating up a Hebrew. Moses jumped in and killed the Egyptian, then quickly buried the body in the sand.

Feeling Like a Failure

The next day, Moses saw two Hebrews fighting. When he asked them to stop, they asked, "Who made you ruler and judge over us?" His own people didn't want to listen to him!

Moses might have dreamed about leading his people out of slavery. But now he wondered if he would ever be a leader.

Escape to Midian

Soon Pharaoh learned that Moses had killed a man. Moses decided to leave Egypt and hide in Midian. He was married there, and got a job working with sheep for his father-in-law, Jethro.

The Amazing Bush

Moses could tell it was on fire. As the sheep grazed, he went to get a closer look.

Why didn't the leaves catch on fire? Why didn't the branches turn black? Moses probably stroked his beard and scratched his head.

Bashful Leader

God spoke to Moses from the bush, and told him to lead the Jews out of Israel. But Moses kept trying to get out of the job. He told God:

1. "I'm nobody special" (Exodus 3:11).
2. "The people won't believe me" (Exodus 4:1).
3. "I'm not a good speaker" (Exodus 4:10).

Objection #3 might have been true. After all, most of Moses' speaking was done to sheep.

Miracles for Moses

God answered all three of Moses' objections.

1. He promised to be with Moses.
2. He showed Moses two quick miracles:
   A. A stick was turned into a snake.
   B. Moses' hand was covered with leprosy—and then the disease disappeared again.

Miracles like these would help the Hebrews listen to Moses.

3. He let Moses take his brother Aaron along to Egypt. Aaron was a good speaker (Exodus 4:14).

Talked Him into It

Wide-eyed Moses decided to forget his shyness and become the leader of Israel.

Didn't Need to Worry

With God's help, Moses became a great leader. He demanded that Pharaoh release the Jews. After God sent ten plagues on Egypt, Pharaoh finally gave in.

Later, with God's help, Moses made a dry path through the Red Sea so the people could cross, and provided water for them in the desert. He judged their disputes.

He also climbed Mount Sinai and received the two stone tablets of the Ten Commandments from God.

Are You Like Moses?

Sandy knew where the neighbors' shovel was. She had watched some boys take it out of the yard and then toss it behind some bushes a block away.

Meanwhile, the neighbors were searching all around. They needed the shovel to dig in their garden. "It looks like we'll have to buy another one," Sandy heard the husband say.

She wanted to help, but it was not easy. Sandy felt shy around adults, and avoided talking to them whenever she could.

However, it would probably cost her neighbors a lot of money to buy a new shovel. That was a waste! Sandy thought it over. Finally, she talked to God about it. If He would help her, she would tell her neighbors, she decided. With shaking knees, Sandy walked next door.

Moses and Sandy did not have the same job, but both felt the same way. It's hard to talk to people and do the right thing when you feel bashful. But with God's help, the job gets a lot easier.

INSTANT RICHES

The men who had leprosy reached the edge of the camp and entered one of the tents. They ate and drank, and carried away silver, gold and clothes, and went off and hid them. They returned and entered another tent and took some things from it and hid them also.

II Kings 7:8

WHAT'S IT ABOUT?

In the midst of a famine, these four men did something brave—and instantly got rich. What would they do next?

★For the whole story, read II Kings 6:24—7:20 in your Bible.

Blockade!

Ben-Hadad, the king of Aram, was trying to conquer the city of Samaria in Israel by siege. His army camped outside the city walls and kept food supplies from getting in. Inside the city, people were starving.

Food Prices Go Up

Food was hard to find in Samaria, and any food that there was became very expensive. A donkey's head sold for eighty shekels of silver, and a half pint of seed pods for five shekels.

Does donkey's head soup sound good to you?

The Officer Snickers

The prophet Elisha told the king of Israel and his officers that in twenty-four hours, everything would change. There would be plenty of food to buy and sell for just a shekel or two.

The officer almost laughed out loud. He said that even if God poured down food from heaven, the situation couldn't improve that quickly!

None for Him

Elisha said again that food would be plentiful—but that the laughing officer wouldn't get any of it.

Four Desperate Men

Meanwhile, four lepers walked up to the camp of the Arameans, planning to surrender to the enemy army. They didn't know whether the enemy would feed them or kill them. But they were already starving and had to try something.

Skin Disease

Today's leprosy, called Hansen's disease, often includes such symptoms as skin lesions and loss of feeling in the hands and feet (making hands and feet prone to injury).

The four may have had leprosy or another disease that affected their skin. They lived outside the city so that no one else would be infected by them.

Population: Zero

When the lepers entered the camp of the Arameans, they found no one home. Everything the enemy owned was left: tents, horses, donkeys, food, treasure. But all the people were gone.

God Tricked Them

God had sent an amazing noise upon the enemy camp. It sounded like a huge army attacking. The soldiers were sure they could hear the rattle of chariot wheels and the thunder of horses' hooves.

Eyes bulging with fear, they ran away, leaving everything.

Easy Pickings

The four lepers were astounded to see food, drink, and clothing as well as silver and gold. They walked from tent to tent, taking whatever they wanted.

Sharing

Suddenly the men realized they couldn't keep all this to themselves. They decided to share their good fortune with those who needed it.

The Suspicious King

When the king heard the news, he found it hard to believe. He thought it was a trick. Maybe the Arameans were waiting near the camp, and would pounce on his people when they left the safety of the city walls.

Send Out the Scouts!

The king sent out two horse-drawn chariots to look for the Arameans. The scouts drove as far as the Jordan River and found clothing and equipment all along the road. The Arameans kept tossing things away as they ran.

Good-bye, Officer

Remember the officer who laughed at Elisha's prophecy of abundant food?

He was on duty at the city gate when the people ran out to the Aramean camp to get food. They were in such a hurry that they knocked the officer down, and he was trampled to death.

It was just as Elisha had said. The officer saw the food, but didn't get to eat it.

Hard to Believe

1. What did the snickering officer find hard to believe?
2. What did the king have trouble believing?

Calculator

1. How many lepers went to the Aramean camp?
2. How many chariots were sent to investigate it?
3. How many Arameans stayed in the camp?

As You See It

What do you feel is the point of this story? Why do you think it was included in the Bible?

THE LOUDMOUTHED BEGGAR

As Jesus approached Jericho, a blind man was sitting by the roadside begging. When he heard the crowd going by, he asked what was happening. They told him, "Jesus of Nazareth is passing by."

He called out, "Jesus, Son of David, have mercy on me!"

Those who led the way rebuked him and told him to be quiet . . . .

Luke 18:35-39a

WHAT'S IT ABOUT?

Everybody told him to stop yelling. What did the blind man do? Was he brave or bashful? Keep reading, and you'll find out.

★You can also read the whole story in your Bible by turning to Luke 18:35-43.

A Bad Road

It was dangerous to travel on the narrow, winding road to Jericho. Often robbers hid along the way, ready to attack travelers.

Collapsing Walls

During the days of Joshua, God had made the walls
of Jericho fall to the ground so that the Israelites
could conquer it. By the time of Jesus, the walls had
been rebuilt.

Roadside Beggars

As Jesus approached Jericho, He came near a beggar
sitting by the road, asking for food or money.

Beggars were plentiful in Israel for several reasons:
1. Disease left many people unable to work.
2. At times jobs were hard to get in Israel.
3. Some people pretended to be blind or crippled in
order to get help from others.

More beggars lived around
Jerusalem than Jericho, because
they could get charity from the
many religious pilgrims visiting
there.

A Walking School

Many rabbis taught as they walked. Jesus probably
did the same thing, sharing with His disciples while
a small crowd tagged along.

Drawing Crowds

The blind man heard the noise of the crowd. Though
he couldn't see anything, he knew something big was
going on. When he found out Jesus was passing by,
he knew he could be healed.

Poor Eyesight

Because of disease, poor sanitation, and inadequate medical care, many people in ancient Israel had trouble with their eyes. Blind beggars would have been common.

Son of David?

The man called out, "Jesus, Son of David, have mercy on me!"

Jesus wasn't David's son; King David had lived and died a thousand years earlier. But the expression "son of" can also mean "descendant of," and Jesus was descended from David.

God had promised that a descendant of David's would be the Messiah (II Samuel 7:12, 13). The blind man believed Jesus was the Messiah (someone special sent by God).

Hush Him Up!

"Shhh! Stop him! Keep him quiet! Put your hand over his mouth!" People didn't want the blind man bothering Jesus.

But the man shouted even more. He wanted Jesus to help him.

Lots of Commotion

Jesus could hear the scuffling as the blind man called out and the people tried to subdue him. Jesus insisted that the man be brought right over. When the blind man came close, Jesus asked what he wanted.

A Gentle Voice

Can you imagine the difference? The blind man was calling out desperately. The crowd was shouting angrily. Maybe Jesus had a gentle, caring voice—just the opposite of all the racket going on.

Short Request

The blind man's request was brief. He wanted to see, and he knew Jesus could help him.

Eight Simple Words

Jesus' reply was short, too. "Receive your sight; your faith has healed you." Yet with that sentence the power of God was released to help the blind man. Pop! He could see.

Telling Everyone

The blind man couldn't wait to tell others what God had done. No one tried to keep him quiet anymore, and he praised God everywhere he went.

Not only had he received his sight, but he was now a follower of Jesus Christ.

In Your Words

1. What is a "walking school"?
2. Why did the crowd want to keep the blind man quiet?
3. Why was Jesus called "Son of David"?

You Be the Detective

Which of these statements are true about Jesus Christ, based on this story?
1. Jesus liked ice cream.
2. Jesus was going to a concert at Jericho.
3. Jesus loves people.
4. Jesus liked to heal.
5. Jesus could speak gently.
6. Jesus liked to read the newspaper.
7. Jesus was related to kings.
8. Jesus charged money for healings.
9. Jesus could give people back their sight just by speaking words to them.

(Answers: 3, 4, 5, 7, 9)

Job Description

The Jews expected the promised Messiah to do certain things. One of these jobs was giving sight to those who were blind physically or spiritually (Luke 4:18, 19). Jesus fit the Messiah's job description because He was the Messiah.

Noisy Critter

If you were the blind man, and people were telling you to be quiet, how would you react? Why?

THE BASHFUL WARRIOR —PART I

The angel of the LORD came and sat down under the oak in Ophrah that belonged to Joash the Abiezrite, where his son Gideon was threshing wheat in a winepress to keep it from the Midianites. When the angel of the LORD appeared to Gideon, he said, "The LORD is with you, mighty warrior."

"But sir," Gideon replied, "if the LORD is with us, why has all this happened to us?" . . .

Judges 6:11-13a

WHAT'S IT ABOUT?

Gideon was hiding from the enemy when God's angel spoke to him. This bashful man did not feel like a mighty warrior, but God had plans for him!

★For the whole story, read Judges 6:1-35 in your Bible.

Secret Weapon

The mean Midianites had been attacking Israel with a new weapon. The Jews had never fought against it before.

What could it be? A huge bag of bees tossed into

the camp? Rolling stones pushed down a hill?

No! It was the dreaded camel.

This was the first time a large number of camels were ever used against Israel in war. These tall, swift "tanks of the desert" must have been a frightening sight.

Camel Necklaces

Many of the Midianites' more fashionable camels wore necklaces shaped like crescent moons. After a battle, the winners took the camel necklaces from the losers as souvenirs.

Stripped Clean

The Midianites were worse than a plague of locusts. Attacking during Israel's harvest time, they stripped the fields of everything. They even killed all the livestock.

1 2 3 4 5 6 7 . . .

The Midianites attacked Israel for seven straight years. Their nasty friends, the Amalekites, came along, too.

Why Were the Jews Losing?

Try to find the answer among the choices below.

1. They couldn't knock the riders off their camels.
2. They hid under their cloaks when the enemy came.
3. The Jews liked to play checkers.
4. The Jews were worshiping false gods.

(Answer: 4.)

Nomads Move In

The Midianites made themselves at home in Israel with their cattle and tents (Judges 6:5). This probably meant their families traveled with the army.

Nomads are groups of people who travel from place to place rather than having a permanent home. The Midianites may have been nomads during part of the year.

Hebrew Hideouts

Because the Midianites attacked so often, the Jews prepared temporary homes in the hills, in caves, and in other shelters. Then, after the Midianites left, the Jews would come out from hiding and return to their land.

Puny Gideon

Try not to laugh. The angel of the Lord appeared to Gideon and called him "mighty warrior." Poor, scared Gideon, hiding in a winepress with a small basket of wheat, must have wondered if this was a joke. What was he going to do, throw wheat at the Midianites?

The Gideon Put-Down

Gideon really felt bad because:
1. He thought God had abandoned Israel.
2. He came from a small family group.
3. He believed he was the least talented person in his family.

Gideon thought he was a loser.

Fast Food Fry

Gideon prepared a meal of meat and bread for his visitor. The angel touched the food with his staff, and *presto!* the rock caught fire. Immediately the meat and bread burned up!

Now Gideon knew this must be an angel from God.

How Much Burned Up?

An ephah of flour weighs about forty pounds. The Israelites had trouble getting enough food, so all this grain—plus a goat, too—was a large offering for Gideon to make.

Cutting Down the Poles

God told Gideon to tear down his father's altar to Baal and the Asherah pole beside it.

Asherah was a false god that many Jews had begun to worship. Part of the worship was centered around a tree trunk or pole. The pole was probably carved or decorated.

Nervous Gideon chopped down the pole at night. He was afraid of being killed if he were discovered.

A New Name

Sure enough, in the morning the men of the town were ready to kill Gideon for breaking down Baal's altar and the Asherah pole. But Gideon's father said that if Baal was really a god, he could punish Gideon himself.

Gideon's new nickname became "Jerub-Baal," which means "Let Baal contend with him" (Judges 6:32).

Round Up an Army

Timid Gideon was gaining courage as he obeyed God. Now he called together an army to fend off a new attack by the Midianites and Amalekites.

Think Back

1. What were the Midianites' secret weapons?
2. What is a nomad?
3. What happened to Gideon's food sacrifice?

(Answers: 1. Camels 2. Nomads are people who wander instead of living in one place. 3. It was burned up.)

Tune in Next Time . . .

At first, Gideon thought he was a loser. But the Spirit of God started making Gideon into a new person.

Do you ever feel like a loser? There's hope!

Tune in to the next page to learn what happens to Gideon.

THE BASHFUL WARRIOR —PART II

Gideon said to God, "If you will save Israel by my hand as you have promised—look, I will place a wool fleece on the threshing floor. If there is dew only on the fleece and all the ground is dry, then I will know that you will save Israel by my hand, as you said."

Judges 6:36, 37

WHAT'S IT ABOUT?

God told Gideon to lead his people in battle. But the bashful warrior wasn't so sure at first!

★For the whole story, read Judges 6:36—7:23; 8:22-27 in your Bible.

Gideon's Knees Knocked

Gideon wanted to obey God, but sometimes he got a little shaky. You can almost hear him trembling as he asks God for a bit of proof that he will win the battle.

Test #1. Gideon put a wool fleece overnight on the floor. He asked that by morning the fleece be wet from the dew, but the ground around it be dry.

Test #2. He left a fleece on the ground again. By morning he wanted the ground wet but the fleece dry.

Positive Proof. God was kind enough to do exactly as Gideon asked both times.

Results. Gideon must have felt that God would help him defeat the enemy.

Explanation Station

What is a fleece?

A fleece is the wool taken from a sheep. There are two types:

1. Wool could be cut off the sheep and then woven together into a soft covering.

2. The skin could be removed from a dead sheep with the wool still in place.

Can an Army Be Too Big?

Gideon rounded up thirty-two thousand men to fight the Midianites. God told him the army was too big. Twenty-two thousand fearful soldiers went home, leaving Gideon only ten thousand.

The Lap Test

God decided the army was still too big. He told Gideon to take the men to the river for a drink of water.

The number of men who knelt down at the riverbank and lapped up the water with their tongues like dogs was 9,700.

Those who scooped up water and drank it from their cupped hands numbered three hundred.

God told Gideon that three hundred men would be plenty to do the job of beating up the Midianites. Everyone else was sent home.

Battle Plan

Divide. Gideon put the men into three groups of one hundred each.

Assign weapons. Each man carried a trumpet and a jar concealing a burning torch.

Take positions. The groups went to three different sides of the Midianite camp.

No Brass Band

The trumpets of Gideon's day were often made from rams' horns rather than from metal, as the trumpets of today.

The Big Surprise

The battle with the Midianites began in the middle of the night, and included three major steps.

Step 1. The Israelites blew their trumpets and smashed their jars.

Step 2. They held up their torches and shouted a battle cry, "A sword for the LORD and for Gideon!"

TOTAL CHAOS

The sleepy Midianites were so frightened
and confused by the noise that they fought
each other with their swords.

Step 3. Those Midianites who escaped the camp
were hunted in the hills by other Jews.

Disappearing Act

The Midianites were defeated so badly that the
nation was never heard of again.

No Crown

Later some of the Israelites pressed Gideon to
become their ruler. (Before this, Israel had had no
ruler except God.) Gideon turned down this honor,
and went back to private living instead.

The Golden Thing

Though Gideon refused to be a
ruler, he did accept thank-you
gifts. He asked each person to
give him a gold earring from the
plunder. He melted the earrings
and made a golden ephod.

We aren't sure what this ephod was or looked like.
But we do know the Israelites turned away from God
and worshiped this golden thing.

Full Circle

Israel was evil.
(Judges 6:1)

Gideon led Israel
to obey God.
(Judges 6:12)

Israel returned
to evil.
(Judges 8:27)

Note the Numbers

1. How many men did Gideon's army originally
have?
2. How many men fought the Midianites with
Gideon?
3. How many "weapons" did each of Gideon's men
carry?

(Answers: 1. 32,000 2. 300 3. A torch, a jar, and a trumpet makes 3.)

Are You Like Gideon?

Would you have given God the fleece tests? Why?
Would you have cut the army down to three
hundred men?
Would you have allowed the Jews to make you
their ruler? Why?
What would you have done with the earrings that
Gideon collected?

(Just give your opinion. There are no wrong answers.)

THE WOMAN WHO STOPPED AN ARMY

David said to his men, "Put on your swords!" So they put on their swords, and David put on his. About four hundred men went up with David, while two hundred stayed with the supplies.

I Samuel 25:13

WHAT'S IT ABOUT?

Someone was in big trouble. David was mad. He had his sword on, and four hundred armed men behind him. Yet one brave woman, Abigail, stopped that army.

★For the whole story, read I Samuel 25:1-42 in your Bible.

On the Run

David and his men were being chased by King Saul, and did not stay in one place long. At the time of this story, David was in the desert near the property of a man named Nabal.

Personality Profiles

Nabal—The Mean Bean
  Assets: owned property
            had 1,000 goats
            had 3,000 sheep
  Problems: nasty personality
              drank too much
              wouldn't listen to advice

Sweet Abigail—Nabal's wife
  Beautiful
    Intelligent
      Good listener
        Protector
          Peacemaker

Sheep Shearing Time

During winter, sheep grow heavy coats of wool.
Once or twice a year, the wool is cut off and used to
make clothing. Usually the sheep's feet are tied to
make the shearing easier.
  Sheep shearing time in Israel was also an occasion
for feasts and celebrations.

David Asks for a Gift

David's protection. While David's men lived in the
desert, they did not steal from Nabal's goods.
Instead they protected the flocks and herds from
robbers (I Samuel 25:15, 16).

David's request. He sent ten men to ask for food from Nabal during this festive time of sheep shearing, as a thank-you for their protection.

Nabal Snaps Back

Grumpy Nabal told the men to take a hike. He made fun of David and refused to give him anything.

Attitude Adjustment

When David heard of Nabal's reply, he told four hundred of his men to put on their swords. They were going to change Nabal's attitude.

Abigail to the Rescue

As soon as Nabal's wife heard what was happening, she set to work to stop David's army. She collected gifts:

    200 loaves of bread
      2 skins of wine
      5 butchered sheep
      5 bushels of grain
    100 cakes of raisins
    200 cakes of pressed figs

Loading the food on donkeys, she hustled off to find David.

Bread is #1

Bread was the major food in the Jews' diet. They seldom ate meat. They used bread like a spoon to scoop up or pick up other pieces of food.

Sh-h-h-h!!

Keep it a secret! Abigail didn't tell irritable Nabal that she was going to see David.

Abigail Apologizes

When she found David, Abigail bowed down and begged for forgiveness on behalf of her family. She explained that her husband was a fool: the name Nabal means fool (I Samuel 25:25).

David Accepts

Abigail's words changed David's mind, and he said:
1. Thanks for coming.
2. You kept me from killing Nabal and his men.
3. Go home in peace (1 Samuel 25:32-35).

The Great Stone Face

When Abigail told Nabal about his close call, his body became stiff. He stared like a stone. After ten days of looking terrible, Nabal died.

Wedding Bells

When David heard of Nabal's death, he sent for the wise and beautiful Abigail and asked her to become his bride. Abigail gathered five maids to assist her and left immediately to marry the dashing David.

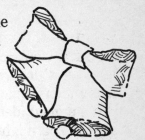

In Your Opinion

Was David right to ask for gifts from Nabal? Why or why not?

Should Nabal have helped David? Why or why not?

Memory Bank

Abigail took six kinds of food gifts to David. Can you name three of them?

(Answers: bread, wine, sheep, grain, raisins, figs)

Computer Check

Match these questions with the right numbers.

1. How many sheep did Nabal own?   5
2. How many men went to ask Nabal for food?   400
3. How many men went to fight Nabal?   10
4. How many maids went to Abigail's wedding?   3,000

(Answers: 1. 3,000 2. 10 3. 400 4. 5)

The Peacemaker

Nabal wasn't looking for peace in his relationship with David. He didn't think about the fact that a food gift would cost him a lot less than a battle! He took the stubborn route. If Abigail hadn't stepped in, many men would have died.

It's a good idea to make peace rather than fight or argue. You might agree to play the game your friend likes, or let your younger brother watch his favorite cartoon. Sometimes you might even offer the larger piece of pie to your sister.

Some people seem to like fighting. Others are like Abigail; they look for ways to solve differences and keep everything peaceful. Jesus said, "Blessed are the peacemakers, for they will be called sons of God" (Matthew 5:9).